THE HOME FRONT

THE BLITZ
EVACUATION
PRISONERS OF WAR
PROPAGANDA
RATIONING
WOMEN'S WAR

Editor: Alison Cooper
Series designer: Nick Cannan
Consultant: Terry Charman, researcher and historian at the Imperial War Museum

First published in 1991 by
Wayland (Publishers) Limited
61 Western Road, Hove
East Sussex BN3 1JD

British Library Cataloguing in Publication Data
Reynoldson, Fiona
The women's war.
1. Great Britain. Women. Social life, history
I. Title II. Charman, Terry III. Series
941.0082

HARDBACK ISBN 0-7502-0011-1

PAPERBACK ISBN 0-7502-0952-6

Typeset by Rachel Gibbs, Wayland
Printed and bound by Casterman S.A., Belgium

CONTENTS

Women at Work

During the First World War, women took over many of the jobs usually done by men, because the men were away fighting. They worked on farms, in munitions factories, on the buses and even in steel mills. They proved that they could do 'men's jobs', as well as the more traditional 'women's work' in nursing and

THESE WOMEN ARE DOING THEIR BIT

LEARN TO MAKE MUNITIONS

Thousands of women worked in munitions factories during the First World War.

From making munitions to making biscuits: women at work in Liverpool in 1926.

domestic service. Many went to work for patriotic reasons. Women's magazines answered many queries like this one:

> 'Seeing my brothers and friends joining the colours, I feel I must do something for my dear old country. I would very much like to go on the land . . . '
> [Reply]: 'You can't do better than go on the land . . . Apply to the Women's National Land Service Corps.'
> (Mrs Marryat, *Woman's Weekly*, 1915.)

When the war ended, the soldiers came home and the women lost their jobs. In the Depression of the 1930s, when many people were unemployed, women continued to be paid less than men and to be kept out of the best jobs. But most women accepted this and saw the man as the family's breadwinner.

> 'I was one of ten and worked all hours as a seamstress for very little money. I married Ted in 1926 and I never had to go out to work again. He gave me the first holiday I'd ever had.' (Lil Lawrence, Kent.)

By 1939, fewer than five million women were working. Two million were in domestic service, with wages as low as 5 shillings (25p) a week. Others worked in factories, shops and offices. The few who entered the professions – teaching, medicine, nursing and the Civil Service – had to leave when they married.

War and Evacuation

The Second World War started in 1939. The government issued everyone with gas masks, in case poisonous gas was dropped on Britain. It knew there would be a shortage of food, so certain foods were rationed to make sure everyone got a fair share. Many women found jobs in the new government food offices in every town and city.

A few days before war was declared, the evacuation scheme started. The Germans had already bombed many European cities and the government expected Britain to be attacked as soon as war broke out. In all,

These evacuees are not wearing labels so they are not part of the government evacuation scheme. Many children were evacuated by their schools or sent to stay with relatives in the country.

Queuing for fruit in the middle of a bomb site. Even ordinary chores such as shopping became difficult during the Blitz.

about three and a half million children and many mothers were moved out of the big cities to save them from the bombing. Anyone with experience of children was called on to help in the journey.

Thousands of women had evacuees staying in their homes in the country. However, many mothers and children were miserable living with strangers. As no bombs fell, the evacuees soon packed their bags and returned home.

Nearly a year later there was a threat of invasion and then bombs did fall on the cities. Women found it terribly hard to decide what would be best for their children.

A child being carried from a bomb site by a warden.

'The children should be taken to the country without asking the parents for the sake of the nation.' (Woman aged forty-five with no children.)
'I'd rather they died with me than be left alone in the world.' (Woman aged sixty with grown-up children.)
'I'm blowed if I'd let my kids go again!' (Woman with young children.)

Evacuation was just the beginning of the disruption that the war was to bring to the lives of many women.

Farm Work and Forestry

The government encouraged women to join the Land Army.

In July 1939 women were called on to help on farms in the event of war. In August 1940 the Women's Land Army had only 7,000 members; by 1943, the number had grown to 77,000.

Women joined the Land Army for all sorts of reasons. Kitty Murphy worked at the Woolwich Arsenal, a factory producing munitions, but she suffered from skin problems. She volunteered for the Land Army for a healthier life. She lived in a farm cottage with no running water, no gas and no electricity but she:

> 'looked a picture of health, living off the fat of the land, jugged hare, pheasant and chicken.' (*A People's War*, Peter Lewis.)

Kitty learnt to milk cows, hoe, hedge, ditch, dig drainage trenches and pick everything from strawberries to sugar beet.

It wasn't a soft job. The women worked a forty-eight-hour week and earned 32 shillings (£1.60).

Many members of the Land Army became forestry workers. These women are cutting pit props for use in coal mines.

'Each time I cleaned out the pigs, I brought up my breakfast. But I soon got over that . . . I changed jobs several times between milking and general farm work on small and large farms. Then I worked with a gang of four girls going round Wiltshire farms with a steam-engine and threshing tackle.' (Land Army worker, quoted in *Love, Sex and War*, John Costello.)

Bringing in the harvest on a farm in Suffolk.

By 1943 there was a severe shortage of people to work in factories and on the land. The government stopped recruiting women into the armed services. Young women had to choose between factory work or joining the Land Army. Most of them made a great success of their jobs.

'I remember three girls from Bootle we put in charge of calves and they were marvellous . . . They became the most efficient tractor drivers . . . They got used to humping potato bags and that sort of thing. I can't think of anything else they couldn't do.' (Sir Emrys Jones, Cultivation Officer, Gloucestershire, quoted in *A People's War*.)

Factory Work and Pay

Thousands of women were needed to work in the factories. They made everything from ammunition and uniforms to aircraft.

'I was going into a huge aircraft factory and I supposed it would be very skilled . . . But there were unskilled men there too . . . so that gave me confidence. We were working from drawings to make the very first Lancaster and I was amazed how many men couldn't read a drawing. I could . . .' (Barbara Davies, quoted in *A People's War*.)

Often factory work meant moving away from home. It meant higher pay and more independence. Many women loved this, although the hours were long and the work hard. Most adapted well to their new jobs.

However good they were at their work, women got less money than men. At the Rolls-Royce factory in Glasgow, women got 43 shillings (£2.15) a week and men got 73 shillings (£3.65) a week for doing exactly the same work. In fact skilled women working big machines were

Working on fuses for shells. These women worked part-time at the factory because they also had homes to run and children to look after.

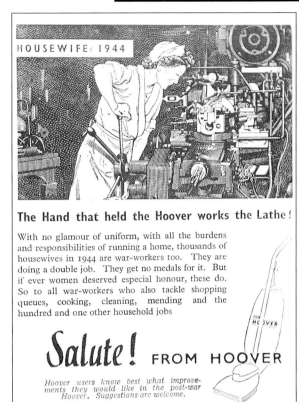

getting less money than the men cleaning the lavatories. At first the women were not used to belonging to trade unions and protesting.

'At work you did exactly as your boss told you and you went home to do exactly what your husband told you.' (Mona Marshall, steelworker, quoted in *A People's War*.)

Things changed at Rolls-Royce in 1943. The women went on strike.

'We were marching along the street, getting eggs and tomatoes thrown at us . . . suddenly the men came marching to support us . . . They were very sympathetic to the women once they realized we were being used for cheap labour! After that women on the big machines got the male semi-skilled rate, but not the skilled rate.' (Agnes Maclean, union shop steward quoted in *A People's War*.)

Above left *Mothers shared the job of looking after young children so that more women could go to work in the factories.*

Above right *Companies such as Hoover had no products to sell during the war. They used advertisements like this one to make sure people would remember their products when the war was over.*

Volunteers

For many women during the war, life was a drab routine of food rationing, clothes rationing, making do, queuing and worrying. Some took over their husband's businesses, working as butchers or bakers, or they worked in shops, factories or offices. Married women had homes to run as well and many stayed at home to bring up young children. Older women and those who could not go out to work full time joined the Women's Voluntary Service (WVS).

The WVS was the largest of all the women's wartime services: it had one million members in 1944. They did all sorts of jobs, from helping with evacuees to distributing stirrup pumps for fire watchers and running canteens at railway stations, on the Underground in London and in bombed-out areas. They drove ambulances, ran nurseries for working mothers and collected scrap metal to be made into aeroplanes. In just one month, the Portsmouth branch of the WVS collected enough scrap metal to fill four railway carriages. Over

A WVS mobile canteen serving rescue workers.

180,000 WVS members ran rest centres for people who had been bombed out of their homes.

Above *Women had to get used to queueing for food.*

'They kept coming in, their bare feet cut and bleeding because they'd walked over glass, the men carrying the children, and only pyjamas on . . . they couldn't believe they'd lost everything.'
(Alice Myers describing a rest centre in Hull, from *A People's War*.)

Below *WVS clothing centres helped people who had lost everything in the bombing.*

WVS work could be far less dramatic.

'My memory of 1943 is being pregnant and sitting with seven or eight other women knitting seamen's stockings, while the small children played with the balls of wool.' (Mary Jones, Oxford.)

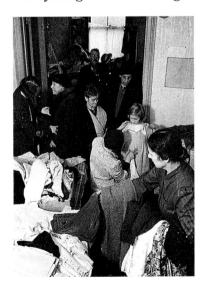

But even in country areas the WVS did not only organize jam-making and knitting. The big cities that were being bombed were not far away and members were sometimes asked to transport supplies of food to areas that had been badly hit.

The Blitz

Towards the end of 1940, the Germans began to launch air raids against British cities. Women carried out many dangerous duties during the Blitz.

The Special Minewatch Units were made up of members of the Women's Royal Naval Service (known as Wrens). When the air-raid siren warned them that enemy bombers were approaching, the Wrens had only two minutes to get to their posts on the bridges across the River Thames.

'When it was our turn for duty we had to sleep fully clothed in shirt, collar and tie and bell-bottoms . . . when awakened by the siren, on went shoes, jackets, tin hat, gas mask over the shoulder and off we would set at a gallop, dashing down the street with guns blasting away and shrapnel pattering down through the branches of the trees.' (Margaret Taylor, quoted in *Women Who Went To War*, Eric Taylor.)

They stood in tiny brick huts looking at the water through slit-shaped windows. They had a 'pointer' to mark the place where they saw anything splashing into the water. They made a note of the place. When the 'All Clear' sounded, one of the Wrens had to run as fast as

Women of the Auxiliary Territorial Service operating a searchlight.

she could to a telephone box, groping in her purse for two pennies (old money). She telephoned the Port of London Authority who closed that stretch of the River Thames until it had been swept for explosive devices such as mines.

Some women became air-raid wardens. Barbara Nixon was one of them.

'I was given a tin hat, whistle and a Civil Defence respirator [gas mask]. The Post Warden took me on a tour of the seventeen public shelters in our area.' (From *Raiders Overhead*, Barbara Nixon.)

Barbara got to know the people in her area, visiting the shelters on her nightly rounds. During very heavy bombing one night, she was blown completely off her bicycle by the blast from an exploding bomb. She picked herself up and carried on.

Above left *London Underground turned off the electricity that ran through the rails at 11 pm every night. People sheltered in the Underground stations during air raids.*

Above right *An air-raid warden at her post.*

Life in the ATS

The women who joined the Auxiliary Territorial Service (ATS) wore khaki-coloured uniform, even down to their underwear. They lived in army Nissen huts or tents if there was no other accommodation available. Their jobs included driving trucks, filling sandbags, digging roads and serving on the searchlight and anti-aircraft gun sites. Like all the other women's services, however, they were not allowed actually to take part in combat. For instance, they could do all the jobs on a gun site except firing the gun.

'First of all you have to recognize the enemy bomber, secondly to know exactly where it is at that moment, thirdly to calculate where it will be in a few seconds time, fourthly to fuse the shell to make it burst at exactly the right moment alongside the bomber.' (Connie Brook, formerly 510 (mixed) Heavy AA Battery, Royal Artillery, from *Women Who Went To War*.)

ATS cooks learn how to prepare meals on an outdoor stove.

At the end of 1941, conscription was introduced for women aged between twenty and thirty and by July 1942 the ATS had 217,000 members.

'The girls who were drafted had a hard time accepting it. Some of them had never been away from home . . . We'd have to get dressed and we'd run and run and march long routes, with packs on our backs and blisters on our heels.' (Joan Savage Cowey, from *Women in War*, Shelley Saywell.)

Some hated life in the ATS because by far the commonest jobs were cooking, cleaning and clerking. However, as the war went on, the number of jobs they were called on to do increased dramatically. To release men to fight, women became armourers, carpenters, draughtsmen, electricians, metalworkers and welders. Many loved their new work.

'I drove a three-ton truck. It was lovely living all that way from home.' (Mary Beck, Coventry.)

Below left *ATS members at work on a gun site.*

Below right *The prime minister, Winston Churchill, ordered this poster to be withdrawn because he thought it made the ATS look too glamorous.*

JOIN THE

ATS

No Flying Allowed

Many girls joined the Women's Auxiliary Air Force (WAAF). They liked the adventurous feel of the Air Force, although sometimes their duties were homely.

'There was an institution at Kenley; a small, warm-hearted WAAF corporal cook, Jean Campbell. Though of much the same age as the sergeant pilots, she took their daily dangers to heart as though they were her sons . . . and when one was missing she would stay up all night if necessary, to welcome him back with a cup of tea.' (from *Ginger Lacey, Fighter Pilot* by R.T. Bickers, quoted in *Women Who Went To War*.)

WAAF workshop hands clean the engines while fabric workers repair the wing of a Wellington bomber.

At other times being a WAAF could be hair-raising. One of the duties of WAAF flight mechanics was to sit on the tailplanes of the Spitfires when they taxied to the runway. One day a pilot forgot to stop and let the WAAF get off.

'I just lay flat down across the whole tail unit and clung on. The control tower made a snap decision that the best thing they could do was not to inform the pilot in case he became too anxious and made a bad landing.' (WAAF Horton, TV interview, quoted in *Women Who Went To War*.)

Luckily he made a perfect landing.

The USSR had three Women's Air Combat Regiments. They were fully operational and the 588th Night Bomber Squadron flew 24,000 sorties. In Britain, however, women were never allowed to fly in combat. Some people wanted to see women as full pilots.

'The WAAF is, I believe, officially recognized as part of the Royal Air Force. It is therefore difficult to see why it should be prohibited [forbidden] from sharing in the latter's essential function, viz: flying.' (Air Chief Marshal Leigh Mallory, quoted in *Women Who Went To War*.)

Above left *A WAAF electrician working on the bomb switch units of a Lancaster bomber in 1943.*

Above right *Princess Mary's RAF nursing service, 1944. Many women nursed in the armed services and in hospitals in Britain.*

Women Pilots

The only women pilots were the air ferry pilots who joined the Air Transport Auxiliary (ATA). They were all women who had learnt to fly before the war. Their job was to ferry aeroplanes from the factories where they were made to the airfields where they were needed.

Eventually 120 of the 820 ATA pilots were women. The accident rate for the women was lower than for the men. But at first they were not very welcome.

'The menace is the woman who thinks that she ought to be flying a high-speed bomber when she really has not the intelligence to scrub the floor of a hospital properly.' (C.G. Grey, editor of the magazine *Aeroplane*, quoted in *The Forgotten Pilots*.)

An ATA instructor with her pupil in 1941.

The first eight women pilots were only allowed to fly Tiger Moths.

Above *ATA pilots in their flying kit.*

'They were open aircraft and their missions were to fly all the way up to Scotland, to Prestwick, which meant four hours or so of flying with a refuelling stop, and they used to come back on the night trains, sitting on their parachutes in the unheated corridors, get into Paddington, out to Hatfield by train, or hitchhike and do the same thing the next day.' (Diana Barnata Walk, ATA pilot, quoted in *Women In War*.)

Soon the eight had proved themselves. More women joined. A flight school was formed where they had lessons on fifteen different types of aeroplane. In the air they were on their own. Many of the aircraft were so new that they did not yet have radios fitted. The ATA pilots had to navigate by map and compass readings and by just looking at the ground.

Jadwiga Pilsudska, a Polish pilot who escaped to Britain and joined the ATA.

The Backroom Girls

A system which used radio waves to detect distant objects such as ships or aircraft was developed just before the war by Robert Watson-Watt. This system became known as radar and it played a vital role in warning of attacks by German aircraft. Many women operated radar systems at bases around the coast of Britain. The Germans bombed these bases time and again.

'The good operator needs a well-developed conscience, a sense of duty, patience and freedom from any tendency to panic. Qualities that women have.' (Sir Robert Watson-Watt, quoted in *Women Who Went To War*.)

Women were involved in other important work behind the scenes. Diana Payne joined the Women's Royal

Below *ATS members plot the course of enemy ships in the English Channel. Their information helped gunners on the coast to find their targets.*

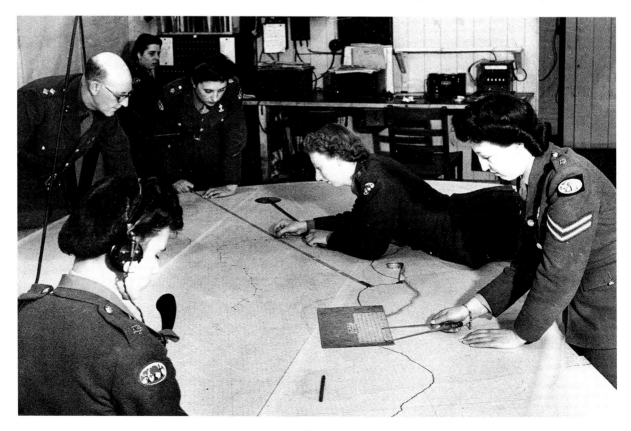

Above *Radio operators taking messages from RAF aeroplanes out on a raid in 1942.*

Naval Service and was selected for a job with Special Duties X. She was sent to a country house near Bletchley Park. It was the Government Code and Cipher School. Diana signed the Official Secrets Act and joined the Ultra team. Their job was to decode German secret messages.

Just before the war the British had got hold of a German Enigma machine, which the Germans used to put all their messages into code. It was rather like an old-fashioned computer. This machine was one of the most important secret weapons of the war, because it enabled the British to read all the German messages. For example, before the battle of El Alamein in North Africa, Hitler sent a message to the German command. The women at Bletchley Park decoded the message and sent it to Montgomery, the British commander. Montgomery received the message before the German command because their decoding machine had got sand in it.

About 2,000 women worked on Ultra. They were all sworn to secrecy until long after the war. They worked long hours and had little free time.

'We were standing up most of the time as it was a big machine, a lumbering, rattling kind of computer . . . The noise was awful.' (June Penny, quoted in *Women Who Went To War*.)

You never know *who's* listening!

CARELESS TALK COSTS LIVES

A poster warns people against talking about anything that might help the enemy.

Top Secret!

Violette Szabo was a member of the Special Operations Executive. She spoke French fluently and in 1944 was parachuted into France to make contact with the Resistance.

'In the secret war against the Nazis, women without number played an invaluable part, participating on terms of perfect equality with men.' (M.R.D. Foot, Special Operations Executive member, quoted in *Women In War.*)

The First Aid Nursing Yeomanry (FANY) drove ambulances and staff cars in battle areas and did some front-line nursing. They had other duties too. Some 2,000 women of FANY worked for the Special Operations Executive, at home and in forty-four other countries from Europe to the Far East. Recruitment could be dramatic.

'I found myself on a train bound for Euston and told to look out there for a tall man wearing a Cambridge Blue rosette.' (Nancy Dawson, quoted in *Women Who Went to War.*)

With other women, Nancy learnt Morse code and ciphers, and how to use teleprinters and wireless sets. The women were then able to receive messages from agents or spies all over the world.

Odette Churchill, pictured here, and Violette Szabo were awarded the George Cross for their work as SOE agents. Both were captured, tortured and imprisoned by the Germans; only Odette survived the war.

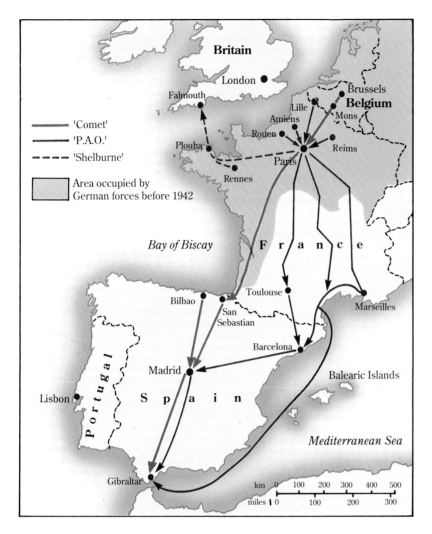

Key:
— 'Comet'
— 'P.A.O.'
- - - 'Shelburne'

Area occupied by German forces before 1942

This map shows some of the escape routes set up in Belgium and France during the war. Allied airmen and people wanted by the Germans were helped along these routes into Spain and on to Britain. The 'Comet' route was run by a Belgian woman, Andrée de Jongh.

Audrey Swithinbank was receiving a message in Morse code when the dots and dashes changed suddenly to a buzz, then broke off. She waited and waited. Later she learned that the agent had been caught at the transmitter by the Gestapo, the German secret police. They had shot him and he had fallen over the Morse keys.

Women were also trained as secret agents. Phyllis Latour, a member of the WAAF, parachuted into German-occupied France. She stayed just behind the coastal defences, radioing back information that helped the Allies to plan the D-Day invasion. Although her house was searched many times, her perfect French, air of innocence and care in hiding her transmitter saved her from being caught.

Keeping Up Morale

Many thousands of men and women were separated from their loved ones during the war. Popular songs such as 'We'll Meet Again' encouraged people to face separation bravely.

'We'll meet again,
Don't know where, don't know when,
But I know we'll meet again
Some sunny day.'

This song was made famous by Vera Lynn. She was a member of ENSA, an organization set up to entertain troops and civilians both at home and abroad. These entertainers, together with film stars such as Margaret Lockwood and Celia Johnson, helped to keep up people's morale during the gloomy years of war.

As the train pulls into a station, soldiers returning from France wave excitedly to their waiting families.

Ann Shelton was a popular singer. Here she is taking part in a radio show broadcast to the British Army in India.

The entry of the USA into the war in 1941 also helped to boost British morale. One and a half million American soldiers came to Britain to prepare for the D-Day invasion. Many began going out with British women, and by May 1944 20,000 British women were married to American soldiers. At the end of the war there were many more who sailed to the USA and a new life.

'The American soldiers were so glamorous; they had plenty of money and most of them were big. Our soldiers in their thick uniforms just didn't compare.' (Jean Pease, Birmingham.)

But despite the glamour of the Americans, there were also plenty of romances among the British forces. Marjorie Bennett was nursing troops suffering from malaria in Sicily when she met and fell in love with an RAF officer. Although nobody knew whether they would survive the war, people continued to get married and have children. They had to assume that life would go on.

The End of the War

When the war in Europe ended in May 1945, there were 460,000 women in the armed services and over six and a half million women in civilian war work. The armed forces were steadily demobilized.

'It was such a relief.' (Joan Gray, Essex.)

It was such a change too. For many women the joy of welcoming back loved ones was overwhelming. But others had to make adjustments of a different kind. Vera Cole was in the ATS. Demobilization lists were put up.

'I saw my name and suddenly realized that my days in the ATS were fast coming to an end . . . Before I left the unit an officer whom I had never seen before, called me over and gave me my conduct sheet on which was written 'exemplary', thanked me, wished me well and said goodbye . . . I was declared fit, my papers stamped 'A1' and told to hand in my kit to the store. I couldn't believe it; all the strict medicals to get into the ATS and there, without even being seen by a doctor, I was out, services no longer required.' (Vera Cole, quoted in *Women Who Went To War*.)

Victory celebrations at the end of the war in 1945.

Private Bill Martin is welcomed home from the Far East by his mother and sisters in 1945.

Wrens studying charts. They worked as river pilots, guiding ships up the River Thames to the docks. Many women missed the comradeship of the armed services when the war was over.

'That was it. The war was over. Back to the home. I found the next few years very hard.' (Jane Brown, Glasgow.)

'No more bombs. We all looked forward to the future.' (Molly McArthur, Glasgow.)

'I missed the comradeship of the Wrens.' (Nan Wilkes, London.)

The war had been an unforgettable experience that had changed everyone. In the years that followed, women were encouraged to go back to work in the home. Some welcomed this with real pleasure, others with reluctance. They had 'done their bit'.

GLOSSARY

All Clear The sound made by the siren that meant the enemy bombers had gone.

Armourers People who make armour e.g. thick metal to protect a lorry or a tank.

Bell-bottoms Wide-legged trousers worn by sailors, that could be easily rolled up.

Ciphers Methods of writing secret messages.

Conscription Being ordered by the government to do war work or join the armed forces.

D-Day invasion The invasion of German-held France by the Allies on their way to defeat Germany.

Demobilized Released from military service.

Domestic service Working for a family as a maid or cook.

Draughtsmen People who make drawings, particularly drawings of machines, aeroplanes etc.

Evacuation scheme The plan to send children out of the cities to safer areas when war came.

Evacuees Children who were evacuated.

Joining the colours Joining a regiment in the army.

Jugged hare A way of cooking a hare in a sort of stew.

Munitions Shells and bullets for guns.

Patriotic Loving your country and feeling a sense of duty towards it.

Seamstress A woman who sews clothes.

Shrapnel Metal chunks from exploding shells and bullets.

Stirrup pumps Small pumps for pumping water to put out fires.

Threshing tackle A machine to separate grains of corn from stalks.

Welders People who join pieces of metal together by melting them at the joints.

PROJECTS

1 Ask older female relatives and friends about the Second World War. Ask them where they were living during the war, whether they went out to work as well as working in the home, how they managed the rations and so on. When you have discovered a few basic facts, ask them if they will tell you more about their wartime experiences.

2 What sort of job would you have liked to do during the war and why? Would you have been allowed to do the job if you were a woman?

BOOKS TO READ

Books for older readers

Caroline Lang, *Keep Smiling Through* (Cambridge University Press, 1990)
Peter Lewis, *A People's War* (Methuen Thames, 1986)
Shelley Saywell, *Women In War* (Penguin, 1986)
Eric Taylor, *Women Who Went To War 1938–46* (Grafton, 1988)
A. Susan Williams, *Women and War* (Wayland, 1989)
Nick Williams, *The Home Front 1939–45* (Macmillan Educational, 1990)

Books for younger readers

Freda Kelsall, *How We Used To Live* (Macdonald/Yorkshire TV, 1987)
Miriam Moss, *A Schoolchild In World War Two* (Wayland, 1988)
Stewart Ross, *A Family in World War Two* (Wayland, 1985)

ACKNOWLEDGEMENTS

The publishers would like to thank the following for permitting us to quote from their sources. (The order of sources is as they appear in the text.) Extracts from Mass-Observation, copyright the Trustees of the Tom Harrison Mass-Observation Archive, reproduced by permission of Curtis Brown Group Ltd. Thames/Methuen for *A People's War* by Peter Lewis, 1986. Pan Books Ltd for *Love, Sex and War* by John Costello, 1985. Grafton Books Ltd for *Women Who Went To War* by Eric Taylor, 1988. Gulliver Publishing Co. Ltd for *Raiders Overhead* by Barbara Nixon, 1980. Penguin Books Canada Ltd for *Women in War* by Shelley Saywell, 1985. Where sources have a name and location only, they were interviewed by the author.

The illustrations in this book were supplied by the following: ET Archive 7 (top), 15 (left); Hulton-Deutsch 5; The Trustees of the Imperial War Museum *cover,* 7 (bottom), 8 (bottom), 10, 11 (left), 12, 13 (bottom), 14, 15 (right), 16, 18, 19, 20, 21, 22, 23 (top), 24 (top), 29 (bottom); Peter Newark's Military Pictures 4, 8 (top), 11 (right), 17, 23 (bottom); Topham Picture Library 6, 9 (top), 13 (top), 24 (bottom), 26, 27, 28, 29 (top). The map on page 25 was drawn by Peter Bull.

INDEX

Numbers in **bold** refer to illustrations.